WORDS OF P
FOR LEADERS

by
John Mason & Tim Redmond

Honor Books
Tulsa, Oklahoma

2nd Printing

Words of Promise for Leaders
ISBN 1-56292-370-6
Copyright © 1997 by John Mason   &   Tim Redmond
                        P. O. Box 54996   P. O. Box 703052
                        Tulsa, Oklahoma 74155   Tulsa, Oklahoma 74170

Published by Honor Books, Inc.
P. O. Box 55388
Tulsa, Oklahoma 74155

All scripture quotations are taken from the *King James Version* of the Bible.

Introduction

The need for leadership is astounding! The world is crying out for strong, character-based leaders who will not wilt or become ineffective in the face of challenging situations. God has the answer to this demand — YOU!

With distinct deliberation, God placed a powerful seed of leadership in your heart before you even knew your name. Your calling to lead is inescapable, and it's time to lean into your destiny and answer your call. God's grace and greatness are inside of you. Let it be felt!

We have written this book to ignite and strengthen your calling as a leader. This carefully selected collection of quotes will serve to inspire you to exercise your leadership in a positive and life-giving way.

It addresses twelve important areas in your life as a leader:

- Character
- Dreams
- Focus
- Associations
- Decisiveness
- Leadership

- Handling Criticism
- Persistence
- Communication
- Mistakes and Failures
- Thought Life
- Passion

As you read this book, expect the leadership seed within you to be watered, nurtured, and energized so you are better equipped to touch the lives of others.

Thanks for the privilege of allowing us to invest in your life.

John Mason & Tim Redmond

CHARACTER

Character is the foundation stone upon which one must build to earn respect. Just as no worthy building can be erected on a weak foundation, so no lasting reputation worthy of respect can be built on a weak character.

R. C. Samuel

*Blessed is a man who can adjust to a set of circumstances
without surrendering his convictions.*

---

*Make sure the thing you're living for
is worth dying for.*

Charles Mayes

CHARACTER

Good character is more to be praised than outstanding talent. Most talents are to some extent a gift. Good character, by contrast, is not given to us. We have to build it piece by piece — by thought, choice, courage and determination.

John Luther

Nearly all men can stand adversity, but if you want to test a man's character, give him power.

Abraham Lincoln

There is always a high cost to low living.

Edwin Louis Cole

One *of the most unselfish things a leader can do*
is to take time to invest in himself.

Tim Redmond

*The result of prayer in private
will be a life of boldness and courage in public.*

Edwin Louis Cole

---

*The study of God's Word, for the purpose
of discovering God's will,
is the secret discipline which has formed the greatest characters.*

James W. Alexander

CHARACTER

The law of harvest is to reap more than you sow.
Sow an act, and you reap a habit;
sow a habit and you reap a character;
sow a character
and you reap a destiny.

G. D. Boardman

The best index to a person's character is:
A) How he treats people who can't do him any good, and
B) How he treats people who can't fight back.

Abigail Van Buren

The size of a leader is determined by the depth of his
convictions, the height of his ambitions,
the breadth of his vision and the reach of his love.

D. N. Jackson

CHARACTER

*K*eep your heart right, especially when it's
sorely wounded.

I would rather be the man who bought the Brooklyn Bridge than the one who sold it.

Will Rogers

———————————

Don't compromise yourself. You're all you've got.

CHARACTER

*Character is power; it makes friends,
draws patronage and support
and opens the way to wealth,
honor, and happiness.*

J. Howe

DREAMS

Some men dream of great accomplishments,
while others stay awake and do them.

Every now and then, bite off more than you can chew.

———————

I believe most people don't know what they can do.

John Mason

DREAMS

Your past is not your potential.

Marilyn Ferguson

*Cherish your visions and your dreams
as they are the children of your soul; the blueprints
of your ultimate achievements.*

Napoleon Hill

---

*Eye hath not seen, nor ear heard, neither have entered into
the heart of man, the things which God hath prepared
for them that love Him.*

1 Corinthians 2:9

DREAMS

God made us, and God is able to empower us to do whatever He calls us to do. Denying that we can accomplish God's work is not humility; it is the worst kind of pride.

Warren Wiersbe

One of the major factors which differentiates
creative people from lesser creative people
is that creative people pay attention to their small ideas.

Roger von Oech

———————————

Plunge boldly into the thick of your purpose.

Some men see things as they are and say, "Why?"
I dream things that never were and say, "Why not?"

George Bernard Shaw

A lot of people owe their success to advice they didn't take.

There are many things that will catch my eye, but there are only a very few that catch my heart; it is those I consider to pursue.

Tim Redmond

DREAMS

The future is so powerful and so full of potential that it only comes one day at a time.

*If you dream big, believe big and pray big,
big things happen.*

———————

*You have never tested God's resources until you have
attempted the impossible.*

God said, "Come to the edge."
We said, "It's too high."
"Come to the edge."
We said, "We might fall."
"Come to the edge."
And we came
and He pushed us.
And we flew.

FOCUS

*The best way to bring focus into your life
is to never place a question mark
where God has put a period.*

John Mason

Focus keeps disappointments from leading us to unbelief.

Jess Gibson

———————————

Losers have tons of variety. Champions take pride in just learning to hit the same old boring winners.

Vic Braden

FOCUS

*A winner knows what to fight for
and what to compromise on.
A loser compromises on what he shouldn't
and fights for what isn't worth fighting about.*

Nothing is as necessary for success as the single-minded pursuit of an objective.

Frederick W. Smith

It isn't that they can't see the solution. It is that they can't see the problem.

G. K. Chesterton

FOCUS

I have so much to do today that I shall spend the first three hours in prayer.

Martin Luther

Learn to recognize the inconsequential, then ignore it.

———————

Most time is wasted, not in hours, but in minutes.
A bucket with a small hole in the bottom gets just as empty
as a bucket that is deliberately emptied.

Paul Meyer

FOCUS

Beware of the lure of the distant and the difficult and deceptive. The great opportunity is where you are.

John Burroughs

If you chase two rabbits, both will escape.

Anonymous

Nothing else, perhaps, distinguishes effective executives as much as their tender loving care of time.

Peter Drucker

FOCUS

Peak performing leaders distinguish between job activities that they can control and those that they can't and they concentrate on what they can do.

Robert Kriegel

When every physical and mental resource is focused, one's power to solve a problem multiplies tremendously.

Norman Vincent Peale

———————

The secret of your future is hidden in your daily routine.

Mike Murdock

F O C U S

It's not so much how busy you are — but why you are busy. The bee is praised. The mosquito is swatted.

Marie O'Conner

It is better to say, "this one thing I do," than to say, "these forty things I dabble in."

Peter Lowe

Whatever you focus your attention upon, you give strength and momentum to.

FOCUS

*I cannot give you the formula for success, but I can give you the formula for failure —
which is: try to please everybody.*

Herbert B. Swope

Men, like nails, lose their usefulness when they lose direction and begin to bend.

Walter Landor

The greater the value, the greater the sacrifice required.

With NO vision, you will perish;
with BLURRED vision, you will be frustrated;
with FOCUSED vision, you will succeed!

Tim Redmond

ASSOCIATIONS

Personal relationships are the fertile soil from which all advancement, all success, all achievement in real life grows.

Ben Stein

*We live up to the expectations that we allow others
to set for us, so be around people
whose expectations are right and high.*

Jim Stovall

---

*If a man does not make new acquaintances as he advances
through life, he will soon find himself alone.
A man should keep his friendships in constant repair.*

Samuel Johnson

ASSOCIATIONS

*L*ook carefully at the closest associations in your life, for that is the direction you are heading.

John Mason

*Associate with people of faith. This tends to be reciprocal.
Your faith will communicate itself to them
and their faith to you.*

Grenville Kleiser

---

*If a loafer isn't a nuisance to you, it's a sign
that you are a bit of a loafer yourself.*

Ed Howe

ASSOCIATIONS

I know you are my friend when you can guard my failures, challenge my thoughts and still celebrate my successes.

T. D. Jakes

My best friend is the one who brings out the best in me.

Henry Ford

Keep away from people who try to belittle your ambitions. Small people always do that, but the really great make you feel that you, too, can become great.

Mark Twain

ASSOCIATIONS

People are lonely because they build walls instead of bridges.

Joseph F. Newton

Be the first to forgive.

If you call one wolf, you invite the whole pack.

Bulgarian Proverb

You can always tell a real friend:
when you've made a fool of yourself
he doesn't feel you've done a permanent job.

Lawrence Peter

The eagle never lost so much time as when he submitted to learn of the crow.

Blake

Wrong associations are people who absorb sunshine and radiate gloom.

*All mentors share two things in common:
1) They believe in you and want to see you succeed.
2) They are willing to offer themselves to you
to assure your success.*

Chip MacGregor

Be slow in choosing a friend, slower in changing.

Benjamin Franklin

———————————

*Keep out of the suction caused
by those who drift backwards.*

E. K. Piper

ASSOCIATIONS

You are the same today that you are going to be in five years from now except for two things: the people with whom you associate and the books you read.

Charlie "Tremendous" Jones

DECISIVENESS

You have to have courage to make a decision and stick with it, knowing that people are going to criticize you no matter what you do.

The secret to becoming confident is preparation.

———————

Action makes more fortune than caution.

Vaulvenargues

*You'll never have all the information you need
to make a decision.
If you did, it would be a forgone conclusion,
not a decision.*

David Mahoney

When you have to make a choice and don't make it,
that in itself is a choice.

William James

———————————

Again and again, the impossible problem is solved
when we see that the problem is only a tough decision
waiting to be made.

Robert Schuller

DECISIVENESS

*It is more important to know where you are going
than to get there quickly.
Do not mistake activity for achievement.*

Abel Newcomer

Expect the unexpected. Nothing ever goes exactly as it seems, but we need to look for unique and unexpected opportunities along our path.

Indecision is debilitating; it feeds upon itself; it is, one might say, habit forming. Not only that, but it is contagious; it transmits itself to others.

H. A. Hopf

DECISIVENESS

Weeds grow lushly in the soil of indecision.

*In order to do an urgent and important work, two things are
necessary: a definite plan and not quite enough time.*

Anonymous

---

*There is a time to let things happen
and a time to make things happen.*

Hugh Prather

DECISIVENESS

Are you a person who says,
"My decision is maybe — and that's final"?

John Mason

*A man's success may depend on his willingness
to make some unpleasant decisions.*

Frank A. Clark

———————

*You seldom get what you go after
unless you know in advance what you want.
Indecision has often given an advantage to the other fellow
because he did his thinking beforehand.*

Maurice Switzer

DECISIVENESS

Our greatest power is the power to choose.

Nothing is as useless as the right answer to the wrong question.

———————————

There's nothing in the middle of the road but yellow stripes and dead armadillos.

James Allen Hightower

DECISIVENESS

*I cannot say whether things
will get any better if they change;
what I can say is that they must change
if they are to get better.*

G. C. Lichtenberg

LEADERSHIP

An uncommon man, the leader. He will do anything to escape the tyranny of mediocrity. He understands that the difference between failure and success is often the difference in doing something nearly right and doing it exactly right. He has the power to persuade and inspire others to heights they thought unreachable.

Unless life is lived for others, it is not worthwhile.

Mother Theresa

---

*Few things in the world are more powerful
than a positive push. A smile. A word of optimism and hope.
A "you can do it" when things are tough.*

Richard DeVos

LEADERSHIP

If *human beings are perceived as potentials*
rather than problems, as possessing strengths
instead of weaknesses, as unlimited
rather than dull and unresponsive,
then they thrive and grow
to their capabilities.

Bob Conklin

Outstanding leaders will go out of their way to boost the self-esteem of their personnel. If people believe in themselves, it's amazing what they can accomplish.

Sam Walton

Believe the best in people before you believe the worst.

Tim Redmond

People are not motivated by failure; they are motivated by achievement and recognition.

F. F. Fournies

People are changed, not by coercion or intimidation, but by example.

People and rubber bands have one thing in common: they must be stretched to be effective.

John Maxwell

High achievement always takes place in the framework of high expectation.

Jack Kinder

A drop of honey catches more flies than a gallon of gall. So with men. If you would win a man to your cause, first convince him that you are his sincere friend. Therein is a drop of honey which catches his heart, which, say what he will, is the highroad to his reason.

Abraham Lincoln

Build a reservoir of good will by placing the interests of your people above your own.

The ultimate leader is one who is willing to develop people to the point that they will eventually surpass him or her in knowledge and ability.

Fred A. Manske, Jr.

First rate people hire first rate people;
second rate people hire third rate people.

Leo Rosten

———————————

There is no limit to what a man can do or where he can go
if he doesn't mind who gets the credit.

The deepest principle in human nature is the craving to be appreciated.

William James

Techniques don't produce quality products or pick up the garbage on time; people do, people who care, people who are treated as creatively contributing adults.

Tom Peters

The leader who never steps on anybody's toes is probably standing still.

LEADERSHIP

Business is a lot like a game of tennis. Those who don't serve well, end up losing.

Doc Anklam

HANDLING CRITICISM

Expecting the world to treat you fairly because you are a good person is a little like expecting a bull not to attack you because you are a vegetarian.

Dennis Wholey

A clear conscience laughs at false accusations.

English Proverb

———————————

Don't waste time responding to your critics.

Any fool can criticize, condemn and complain, and most do.

Dale Carnegie

A critic is a man who knows the price of everything and the value of nothing.

Oscar Wilde

Men are not against you; they are merely for themselves.

Jean Fowler

The stones that critics hurl with harsh intent
a man may use to build his monument.

Arthur Guiterman

*I would have never amounted to anything
were it not for adversity.*

J. C. Penney

---

*The first and great commandment about critics is:
don't let them scare you.*

Elmer Davis

HANDLING CRITICISM

Honest criticism is hard to take, particularly from a relative, a friend, an acquaintance, or a stranger.

Franklin P. Jones

If revenge is sweet, why does it leave such a bitter taste?

---

*If you are not big enough to stand criticism,
you are too small to be praised.*

Anonymous

*To avoid criticism,
do nothing, say nothing,
be nothing.*

Elbert Hubbard

Adversity causes some men to break;
others to break records.

William A. Ward

When I am angry at myself, I criticize others.

Ed Howe

HANDLING CRITICISM

The problem with most of us is we would rather be ruined by praise than saved by criticism.

Norman Vincent Peale

It's one hundred times easier to criticize than create.

Lloyd Cory

———————————————

Not every word requires an answer.

*One of the burdens of success
is to be unpopular when necessary.*

PERSISTENCE

A determined soul will do more with a rusty monkey wrench than a loafer will accomplish with all the tools in a machine shop.

Rupert Hughes

90% of all failures result from people quitting too soon.

---

*Many people are like a wheelbarrow —
they go no further than they are pushed.*

*You can't build a reputation
on what you're going to do.*

Henry Ford

There's a difference between interest and commitment. When you're interested in doing something, you do it only when it's convenient. When you're committed to something, you accept no excuses, only results.

Kenneth Blanchard

———————

We are judged by what we finish, not by what we start.

*B*e thankful for problems, for if they were
less difficult, someone with less ability
would have your job.

God grant me the courage not to give up what I think is right even though I think it is hopeless.

Admiral Chester Nimitz

High achievers don't do what they want to do but do what needs to be done.

Bob Harrison

PERSISTENCE

The impossible is often the untried.

Jim Goodwin

It is good to dream, but it is better to dream and work. Faith is mighty, but action with faith is mightier. Desiring is helpful, but work and desire are invincible.

Thomas Gaines

Become famous for finishing important, difficult tasks.

There is a fine difference of perspective between getting involved and being committed. In ham and eggs, the chicken is involved, but the pig is committed.

John A. Price

*The world will always give you the opportunity to quit,
but only the world would call quitting an opportunity.*

Clint Brown

---

*We can do anything we want to do
if we stick to it long enough.*

Helen Keller

*You may have to fight a battle
more than once to win it.*

Margaret Thatcher

If the dream is big enough, the facts don't count.

Dexter Yager

───────────────

You can judge a leader by the size of the problems he tackles — people nearly always pick a problem their own size, and ignore or leave to others the bigger or smaller ones.

Anthony Jay

PERSISTENCE

*A*ny diamond will tell you that they are just a
hunk of coal that stuck to their job
and made good under pressure.

COMMUNICATION

The most important words in the English language:
5 most important words: <u>I am proud of you!</u>
4 most important words: <u>What is your opinion?</u>
3 most important words: <u>If you please.</u>
2 most important words: <u>Thank you.</u>
1 most important word: <u>You.</u>

Anonymous

*Most conversations are simply monologues
delivered in the presence of a witness.*

Margaret Millar

---

*Nine-tenths of the serious controversies that arise in life
result from misunderstanding, from one man not knowing
the facts which to the other man seem important,
or otherwise failing to appreciate
his point of view.*

Justice Louis D. Brandeis

COMMUNICATION

Listen, Listen, Listen — and then consider speaking (in that order).

Tim Redmond

Sign under a mounted fish: "I wouldn't be here
if I didn't open my big mouth!"

———————

When the employees no longer believe that their manager
listens to them, they start looking around
for someone who will.

COMMUNICATION

*B*e still when you have nothing to say;
when genuine passion moves you,
say what you've got to say, and say it hot.

D. H. Lawrence

Some people speak from experience;
others, from experience, don't speak.

———————————

Drawing on my fine command of the English language,
I said nothing.

Robert Benchley

COMMUNICATION

Laughter is the shortest distance between two people.

Victor Borge

When God tells you to do something, do you talk back?

———————

Don't put people down — unless it's on your prayer list.

Stan Michalski

Seek first to understand, then to be understood. Most people do not listen with the intent to understand; they listen with the intent to reply.

Stephen R. Covey

MISTAKES & FAILURES

Failure should challenge us to new heights of accomplishment, not pull us to new depths of despair. Failure is delay, but not defeat. It is a temporary detour, not a dead-end street.

William Ward

I would rather fail in a cause that will ultimately succeed than succeed in a cause that will ultimately fail.

Woodrow Wilson

_____

There's only one thing more painful than learning from experience, and that is not learning from experience.

MISTAKES & FAILURES

The man who makes no mistakes lacks boldness and the spirit of adventure. He never tries anything new. He has a brake on the wheels of progress.

M. W. Larmour

*The single most important difference
between champion achievers and average people
is their ability to handle rejection and failures.*

Tom Hopkins

———————————

*Failure is only the opportunity
to begin again more intelligently.*

Henry Ford

MISTAKES & FAILURES

*E*ach problem has hidden in it an opportunity
so powerful that it literally dwarfs the problem.

Joseph Sugarmen

Growth is the process of responding positively to change.

---

*In times like these it helps to recall
that there have always been times like these.*

Paul Harvey

MISTAKES & FAILURES

More men fail through lack of purpose than lack of talent.

Billy Sunday

Don't fear failure so much that you refuse to try new things.
The saddest summary of life contains three descriptions:
could have, might have, and should have.

Louis Boone

It is the height of absurdity to sow little but weeds
in the first half of one's lifetime
and expect to harvest a valuable crop
in the second half.

Percy Johnston

MISTAKES & FAILURES

People are not remembered by how few times they fail, but by how often they succeed. Every wrong step is another step forward.

Thomas Edison

One of the most frequent causes for failure of able-bodied men is impatience in waiting for results.

———————————

If your project doesn't work, look for the part that you didn't think was important.

Arthur Bloch

MISTAKES & FAILURES

*The man who has never made a mistake
will never make anything else.*

George Bernard Shaw

THOUGHT LIFE

*Vision is the world's most desperate need.
There are no hopeless situations,
only people who think hopelessly.*

Winifred Newman

Every human mind is a great slumbering power until awakened by a keen desire and definite resolution to do.

Edgar Roberts

———————————

A hungry heart is like a parachute. When you pull on it, it opens up and it saves you.

Joel Budd

Do not think that what your thoughts dwell upon is of no matter. Your thoughts are making you.

Bishop Steere

Attitudes alter abilities.

---

*There is no money problem — it's always an idea problem.
So think longer.*

Robert Schuller

Prayer is powerful. The devil smiles when we make plans. He laughs when we get too busy. But he trembles when we pray.

Corrie Ten Boom

Never complain about what you permit.

Mike Murdock

─────────────

He who angers you, conquers you.

Elizabeth Kenny

The person who knows "how"
will always have a job.
The person who knows "why"
will always be his boss.

Diane Ravitch

*What is the difference between an obstacle
and an opportunity?
Our attitude toward it.*

J. Sidlo Baxter

———————

*You will become as small as your controlling desires;
as great as your dominant aspiration.*

James Allen

THOUGHT LIFE

Think positively about yourself, keep your thoughts and actions clean, ask God who made you to keep on remaking you.

Norman Vincent Peale

PASSION

Only passion, great passion, can elevate the human soul to achieve great things.

Denis Diderot

*A man can succeed at almost anything
for which he has unlimited enthusiasm.*

Charles Schwab

---

*After he had finished a concert and gone back stage,
Fritz Kreisler heard someone say,
"I'd give my life to play as you do!"
He turned and looked at the lady and said,
"Madam, I did."*

PASSION

If a man is called to be a street sweeper, he should sweep streets even as Michelangelo painted, or Beethoven composed music, or Shakespeare wrote poetry. He should sweep streets so well that all the hosts of heaven and earth will pause to say, "here lived a great street sweeper who did his job well."

Martin Luther King, Jr.

When was the last time someone said "Wow!"
after interacting with you?

Tim Redmond

Great spirits have always encountered
violent opposition from mediocre minds.

Albert Einstein

PASSION

He did it with all his heart, and prospered.

2 Chronicles 31:21b

How many feasible projects have been miscarried through despondency and been strangled in their birth by a cowardly imagination?

Jeremy Collier

He who has lost confidence can lose nothing more.

Boiste

PASSION

Make no little plans.
They have no magic to stir men's blood.
Make big plans: aim high!

D. H. Burnham

Optimism is the faith that leads us to achievement.
Nothing can be done without hope and confidence.

Helen Keller

———————————

Remember, it's passion that persuades.

PASSION

*Strong lives are motivated by dynamic purposes;
lesser ones exist on wishes and inclinations.
The most glowing successes
are but reflections of an inner fire.*

Kenneth Hildebrand

*Confidence is when you care enough
to send the very best
and you go yourself.*

Robert Orben

---

*Success is not the result of spontaneous combustion.
You must set yourself on fire.*

Reggie Leach

PASSION

Our business in life is not to get ahead of others, but to get ahead of ourselves — to break our own records, to outstrip our yesterday by our today, to do our work with more force than ever before.

Stewart B. Johnson

Success is a trendy word.
Don't aim for success if you want it;
just do what you love and it will come naturally.

David Frost

About The Authors

John Mason is the author of many best-selling titles which include *An Enemy Called Average*, *You're Born An Original — Don't Die A Copy!*, *Let Go of Whatever Makes You Stop*, *Conquering An Enemy Called Average*, and *Ask*, among others. He is a nationally recognized speaker at both churches and conferences. For more information about seminars, consulting services, or to write the author, please send your correspondence to:

John Mason
P. O. Box 54996
Tulsa, OK 74155

Tim Redmond is the Executive Vice President of the rapidly growing Tax & Accounting Software Corporation, co-author of *Words of Promise for Men*, and is a popular speaker to business and ministry leaders nationwide. For more information about seminars, consulting services, or to write the author, please send your correspondence to:

Tim Redmond
P. O. Box 703052
Tulsa, OK 74170